EAGLE OWL

GREAT GRAY OWLS

Some owls

live in trees.

Owls fly

without making
a sound.

Barn owl

Barn owls

Owls are

awake at night.

Owls are

good at hiding.

SCREECH OWL

GOLDEN EAGLE

Eagles spread

their wings
out wide.

Eagles can see

very far away.

BALD EAGLE

BALD EAGLE

Eagles swoop

down.

Eagles fly

way up high.

BALD EAGLE

BLACK EAGLE

Eagles rest

in nests.

Eagles and owls don't really hang out together. Eagles are diurnal, which means they are active during the day, and owls are nocturnal, which means they are active at night.

2

1

3

Find the Hidden Birds

The owls and eagles you see here can be found repeated in earlier pages of this Ranger Rick Zoobies. Can you match up these birds **1-2-3-4-5** with their twins hiding elsewhere in Ranger Rick Zoobies?

Plus, use the bird illustrations throughout this book to help your child learn to count!